CLEAN WATER

IN INFOGRAPHICS

Envir💡Graphics

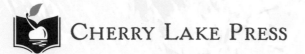

Published in the United States of America by Cherry Lake Publishing Group
Ann Arbor, Michigan
www.cherrylakepublishing.com

Reading Adviser: Marla Conn, MS, Ed., Literacy specialist, Read-Ability, Inc.
Photo Credits: ©Clker-Free-Vector-Images/Pixabay, cover; ©OpenClipart-Vectors/Pixabay, cover;
©OpenIcons/Pixabay, cover; ©UnboxScience/Pixabay, cover; ©Shutterstock, cover; ©Shutterstock,
1; ©Luxteria/Pixabay, 5; ©Shutterstock, 5; ©Shutterstock, 6; ©Shutterstock, 7; ©Shutterstock, 8;
©Shutterstock, 10; ©Shutterstock, 11; ©Shutterstock, 12; ©Shutterstock, 13; ©artbesouro/iStock/
Getty Images, 14; ©Shutterstock, 15; ©OpenClipart-Vectors/Pixabay, 17; ©Shutterstock, 17;
©Shutterstock, 19; ©Shutterstock, 20; ©Shutterstock, 21; ©Shutterstock, 21; ©Shutterstock, 24;
©Shutterstock, 25; ©Shutterstock, 26; ©Shutterstock, 26; ©Luxteria/Pixabay, 27; ©Shutterstock,
27; ©Shutterstock, 28; ©Shutterstock, 29; ©Ariel Skelley/DigitalVision/Getty Images, 30

Cherry Lake Press is an imprint of Cherry Lake Publishing Group.

Library of Congress Cataloging-in-Publication Data has been filed and is available at catalog.loc.gov

Cherry Lake Publishing Group would like to acknowledge the work of the
Partnership for 21st Century Learning, a Network of Battelle for Kids. Please
visit http://www.battelleforkids.org/networks/p21 for more information.

Printed in the United States of America
Corporate Graphics

TABLE OF CONTENTS

What Is Clean Water?

About 70 percent of Earth's surface is covered in water. Most of it is saltwater or frozen in glaciers. Very little is usable by humans. Clean water is needed to live a healthy life. This includes drinking, bathing, and growing food. Many people do not have access to clean water. Sometimes, the water is polluted. Other times, it has all been used up. There are many efforts around the world to keep Earth's water clean and accessible.

WATER ISSUES

1 gallon of gasoline can pollute
750,000 GALLONS
(2.8 million liters) of water.

A 2017 report found that **3 IN 10** people do not have access to safe drinking water at home.

Close to **3 BILLION** people can't wash their hands at home.

2000

2017

Between 2000 and 2017, global efforts increased safe drinking water access from **61%** to **71%** of people.

CHAPTER 1

Water on Earth

Water can be found in many places. It is in oceans, rivers, and lakes. It falls from the sky and flows underground. But there is a small amount of fresh, clean water available for humans to use.

WATER AND EARTH

Water expands by **9%** when it freezes.

There are about
326 QUINTILLION GALLONS
(1,234 quintillion liters)
of water on Earth.

Close to **70%** of Earth's freshwater is trapped in glaciers.

WATER AND PEOPLE

Humans can only use **0.007%** of the water on Earth. The rest is frozen or too salty.

The human brain is **75%** water.

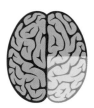

A human can go about **30 DAYS** without food but only a few days without water.

A tree is **75%** water too.

THE WORLD'S WATER RELATIVE TO THE SIZE OF EARTH

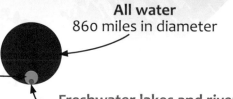

Earth
7,917.5 miles* in diameter

All water
860 miles in diameter

Fresh liquid water in the ground,
lakes, swamps, and rivers
169.5 miles in diameter

Freshwater lakes and rivers
34.9 miles in diameter

1 mile = 1.6 kilometers

LOCATIONS OF WATER

Water Source	Percent of Freshwater	Percent of Total Water
Oceans, seas, and bays	0	96.54
Ice caps, glaciers, and permanent snow	68.7	1.74
Groundwater	30.06	1.69
Ground ice and permafrost	0.86	0.022
Lakes	0.26	0.013
Soil moisture	0.05	0.001
Atmosphere	0.04	0.001
Swamp water	0.03	0.0008
Rivers	0.006	0.0002

THE WATER CYCLE

PRECIPITATION

SNOWMELT

LAKE

RIVER

UNDERGROUND
WATER

WATER MOLECULES

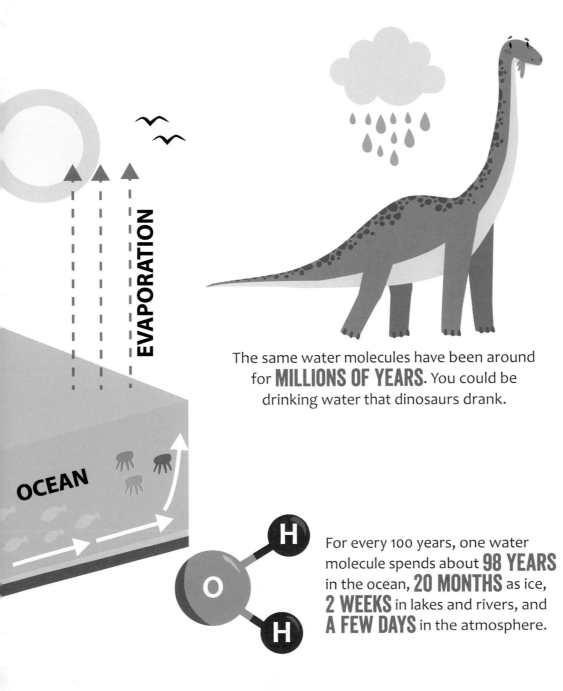

EVAPORATION

OCEAN

The same water molecules have been around for **MILLIONS OF YEARS**. You could be drinking water that dinosaurs drank.

For every 100 years, one water molecule spends about **98 YEARS** in the ocean, **20 MONTHS** as ice, **2 WEEKS** in lakes and rivers, and **A FEW DAYS** in the atmosphere.

CHAPTER 2

Water and People

All living things need water to thrive. Without clean water to drink, people can get very sick. Clean water is not just used for drinking. It is also used for **sanitation**. This includes clean water for bathing, washing hands, and flushing toilets. Water is also needed for **agriculture** around the world. Some countries use the majority of their clean water for food production.

HUMANS ARE MADE OF MOSTLY WATER

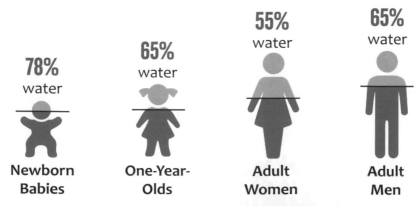

78% water
Newborn Babies

65% water
One-Year-Olds

55% water
Adult Women

65% water
Adult Men

[21ST CENTURY SKILLS LIBRARY]

WATER HELPS THE BODY . . .

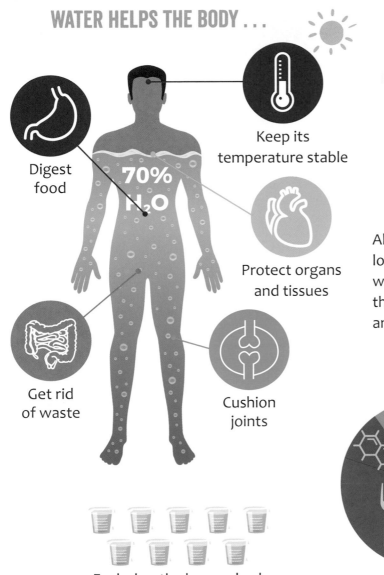

70% H₂O

Digest food

Keep its temperature stable

Protect organs and tissues

Get rid of waste

Cushion joints

Each day, the human body loses **9 CUPS** (2.1 liters) of water.

About **64%** of water loss is through bodily waste. The rest is through breathing and sweating.

About **60%** of water intake is through drinking and about **30%** is from food. The rest is made by cells in the body.

WITHOUT ENOUGH WATER

⧗ Short-Term	📅 Long-Term
Dehydration	Dry skin
Weakness	Tiredness
Dizziness	Headaches
Confusion	Growth problems
	Brain problems

AS OF 2016 . . .

1 BILLION PEOPLE do not have access to clean drinking water.

2 BILLION PEOPLE do not have access to toilets.

3 BILLION PEOPLE worldwide do not have a place to wash their hands at home.

2016, United Nations

PERCENT OF FRESHWATER USED FOR AGRICULTURE

13%
United Kingdom

20%
Russia

36%
United States

64%
China

76%
Mexico

90%
India

99%
Somalia

2016, World Bank

WATER NEEDED TO PRODUCE...

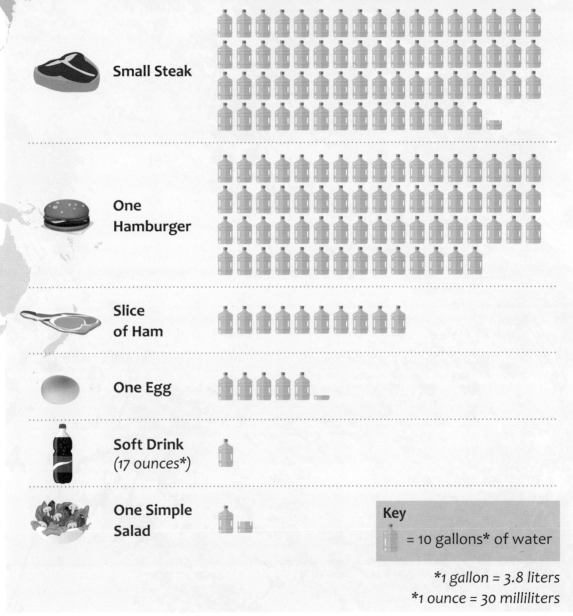

Small Steak

One Hamburger

Slice of Ham

One Egg

Soft Drink (17 ounces*)

One Simple Salad

Key

= 10 gallons* of water

*1 gallon = 3.8 liters
*1 ounce = 30 milliliters

2017, Grace Communications Foundation

CHAPTER 3

Clean Water Issues

Some countries use more water than others. People often use more water than they need. This is called overconsumption. Humans also pollute clean water. Pollution can make water unsafe for people and animals to use. Humans are not the only living things that depend on clean water. Animals need water for drinking, bathing, and food as well.

WATER USE IN THE UNITED STATES

100,000 GALLONS* of water are used in the average home each year, as of 2016.

A family of four can use up to **26,000 GALLONS** each year to flush their toilets, according to a 2019 article.

*1 gallon = 3.8 liters

3,000 GALLONS of water can be wasted by one leaky faucet in one year.

TOP WATER USERS

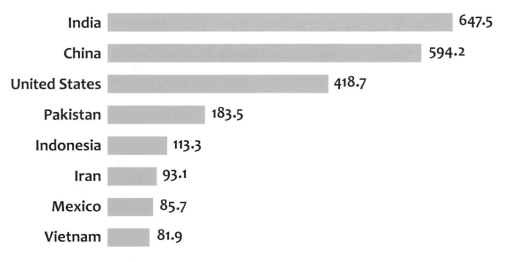

Country	Water Per Year (billion cubic meters)
India	647.5
China	594.2
United States	418.7
Pakistan	183.5
Indonesia	113.3
Iran	93.1
Mexico	85.7
Vietnam	81.9

Water Per Year *(billion cubic meters)*

2019, World Bank

HOW WATER GETS POLLUTED

Industry

Toxins are released from as much as **7.6 BILLION TONS** of industrial waste each year, as of 2016.

Sewage and Wastewater

A 2017 study found that more than **80%** of wastewater flows into rivers or oceans without proper treatment.

FACTS

Since 2014, three-quarters of Americans live within **10 MILES** (16 km) of polluted water.

1 BILLION PEOPLE get sick from contaminated water every year, as of 2018.

Diseases that spread through water include **CHOLERA, GIARDIA,** and **TYPHOID**.

Agriculture

Chemicals can **contaminate** lakes, rivers, and groundwater. As of 2017, an estimated **500,000 TONS** of pesticides are used each year in the United States.

Garbage

Since 2017, nearly **140 MILLION TONS** of **municipal** garbage go to landfills each year in the United States. Landfills can leak into groundwater.

YEARLY CASES

Cholera
1.4–4 MILLION

Typhoid
11–20 MILLION

Giardia
200 MILLION

2016, World Health Organization; 2018, World Health Organization; 2000, Environmental Protection Agency

WATER POLLUTION HOTSPOTS

United States: Ohio River

Source: Industrial waste, agricultural runoff

Result: Pollution creates toxic conditions for plants, animals, and humans.

Afghanistan

Source: Sewage, industrial waste

Result: In 2018, more than 80 percent of water available for human use was contaminated.

Uganda, Tanzania, Kenya: Lake Victoria

Source: Sewage, industrial waste, agricultural runoff

Result: Toxic conditions for fish. Millions of people do not have access to clean water.

India: Ganges River

Source: Sewage, chemicals

Result: It is called the world's most polluted river and is the source of many waterborne diseases.

POLLUTION

As of 2015, plastic pollution kills **1 MILLION** seabirds and **100,000** sea mammals every year.

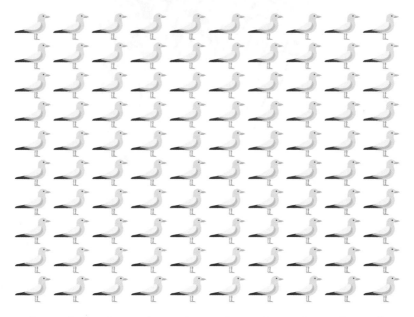

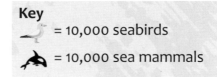

Key

 = 10,000 seabirds

= 10,000 sea mammals

A **dead zone** in the Gulf of Mexico covers more than **8,000 SQUARE MILES** (20,720 square kilometers), as of 2019.

AGENTS OF POLLUTION

Litter

- Garbage is dumped or blows into water.
- Animals can get caught in pieces of trash.
- If eaten, the garbage can cause animals to die.

Acid Rain

- Chemicals mix with water in the air.
- They create acid rain.
- It builds up in water, hurting and killing fish.

Mercury

- Mercury is released by industrial waste.
- It builds up in the bodies of fish.
- When eaten, these fish can poison humans and other animals.

Pesticides and Fertilizers

- Chemicals run off into waterways.
- Oxygen and **pH** levels are changed.
- This can cause dead zones.

CHAPTER 4

Fixing the Problem

Around the world, thousands of groups work to help people access clean water. The World Bank and the United Nations are two of the largest. There are also many things people can do around their homes to help conserve water.

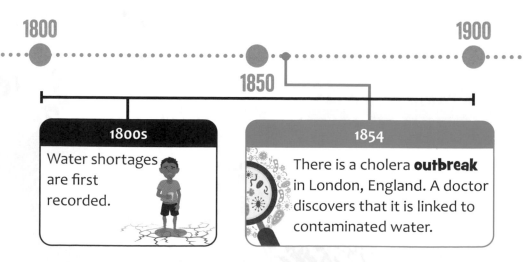

1800

1850

1900

1800s

Water shortages are first recorded.

1854

There is a cholera **outbreak** in London, England. A doctor discovers that it is linked to contaminated water.

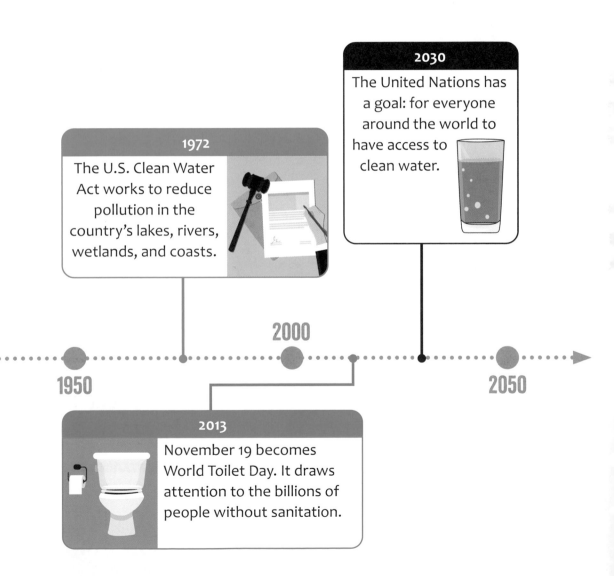

1972

The U.S. Clean Water Act works to reduce pollution in the country's lakes, rivers, wetlands, and coasts.

2030

The United Nations has a goal: for everyone around the world to have access to clean water.

2000

1950

2050

2013

November 19 becomes World Toilet Day. It draws attention to the billions of people without sanitation.

CLEAN WATER SUCCESS STORIES

Massachusetts, United States
Charles River

Issue: Every year, rain washed 1.7 billion gallons (6.4 billion liters) of sewage and stormwater into the river. The river was unsafe for human use.

Clean Water Group: Environmental Protection Agency and local groups

Effort: Sewer and stormwater systems were improved.

Result: In 2013, people could swim in the river for the first time in 60 years.

Honduras
Solimar de Zepeda

Issue: Sanitation and hygiene

Clean Water Group: Pure Water for the World

Effort: Education on hygiene and water use, installation of water filters and bathrooms

Result: Thousands of people gained access to clean water, including a bathroom at the school.

Yemen
Swamp in Harran

Issue: The swamp was contaminated by sewage, increasing the local risk of cholera.
Clean Water Group: United Nations Children's Fund

Effort: In 2017 and 2018, new sanitation systems were installed.

Result: 20,000 people benefited. This inspired similar projects in other parts of the country.

[21ST CENTURY SKILLS LIBRARY]

WHAT YOU CAN DO

Turning off the tap while brushing your teeth can save **8 GALLONS*** of water a day.

Taking a 10-minute shower instead of a bath can save **10 TO 25 GALLONS** of water.

Only running the dishwasher when it is full can save more than **300 GALLONS** of water a year.

*1 gallon = 3.8 liters

2019, World Bank

Activity

JOIN A CLEAN WATER WORKING GROUP

Take action to help with local clean water efforts. Find a group near you that is working to improve water issues.

1. Use a map or the internet to look at your area. What large bodies of water are nearby? What about smaller water sources, such as streams and ponds?

2. Check local newspapers or the internet for local water issues. Are there problems with pollution or overuse?

3. Find out how you can help. Use the internet to find a local water group. Lakes, streams, rivers, and coasts usually have special action groups. They hold many cleanup efforts.

4. Volunteer to help at the next cleanup event!

Learn More

BOOKS

Hunt, Santana. *The Water Cycle*. New York, NY: Gareth Stevens Publishing, 2020.

Labrecque, Ellen. *Clean Water*. Ann Arbor, MI: Cherry Lake Publishing, 2018.

Yomtov, Nelson. *Water/Wastewater Engineer*. Ann Arbor, MI: Cherry Lake Publishing, 2015.

WEBSITES

Precipitation Education
https://pmm.nasa.gov/education/water-cycle

Water Science School
https://www.usgs.gov/special-topic/water-science-school

WaterSense for Kids
https://www.epa.gov/watersense/watersense-kids

BIBLIOGRAPHY

National Geographic. "Freshwater Crisis." Last modified August 20, 2019. https://www.nationalgeographic.com/environment/freshwater/freshwater-crisis

Unicef. "Progress on Drinking Water, Sanitation and Hygiene 2000–2017." https://www.unicef.org/reports/progress-on-drinking-water-sanitation-and-hygiene-2019

The World Bank. "The World Bank Maps." https://maps.worldbank.org

World Health Organization. "Drinking-water." Last modified June 14, 2019. https://www.who.int/news-room/fact-sheets/detail/drinking-water

World Wildlife Fund. "Threats: Pollution." https://www.worldwildlife.org/threats/pollution

GLOSSARY

agriculture (ag-ruh-KUHL-chuhr) the job of farming or the science of improving farming methods

atmosphere (AT-muhss-feer) the layer of gases that surrounds Earth

contaminate (kuhn-TA-mi-nayt) to make dirty or dangerous by adding harmful materials

dead zone (DED ZOHN) an area of water that does not have enough oxygen to support aquatic life

dehydration (dee-hy-DRAY-shun) a type of sickness due to a lack of water in the body

municipal (myoo-NISS-euh-puhl) having to do with the government of a city or town

outbreak (OWT-brayk) a sudden rise in the number of people who are sick from a particular illness

pH (PEE-AYCH) a scale from 0 to 14 that tells how acidic something is

sanitation (san-uh-TAY-shun) the process of protecting people from dirt and disease by keeping places clean

INDEX

ABOUT THE AUTHOR

Renae Gilles is an author, editor, and ecologist from the Pacific Northwest. She has a bachelor's degree in humanities from Evergreen State College and a master's in biology from Eastern Washington University. Renae and her husband live in Washington with their two daughters, Edith and Louisa.